1st Book Edition from the

" I'll Be Brief " Series

" Read with ease and understanding "

Arnell Lane Hall

Victoria E. Kain

The "I'll Be Brief " Series Overview

Arnell Lane Hall, aka Victoria E. Kain, introduces the "I'll Be Brief" Series and its first publication "Do You Know C.P.R..?" This book offers a straight talk approach to Cultivating Professional Relationships in the 21st Century Workplace. All Books in the "I'll Be Brief" Series can be identified by their stunning graphic illustrations and ease of reading, allowing readers the ability to take time and "enjoy" reading in this fast paced and busy life we live.

The "I'll Be Brief" Series will offer a variety of book titles that will be written by different Author's across all genres including, Business Guides, Self Help books, Children's books, Fiction, Non-fiction, Poetry, Mystery, Comedy, Documentaries and more. All books in the Series are rated **"A" for Anyone**! Another key feature of books in this Series is, they can be read in only a day!

Having said that, we hope you will enjoy reading this book and all others from this line. As promised at the onset of this overview, "I'll Be Brief."

"DO YOU KNOW C.P.R.?"
Cultivating **P**rofessional **R**elationships

The above book title was first published in California, and may be available for purchase at Barnes & Noble, Walmart, Amazon, Itunes, Kindle or through other Distributors. Due to promotion or regional zoning, this title may not be immediately available at your favorite retail store. You may contact Fycore Publishing to order copies or additional copies in other formats. Organizations with orders exceeding more than 100 copies will have a 90 day net Invoice available.

"Do You Know C.P.R.?" is available in these formats:

CD (Audio Book)	$14.95
Soft Back	$13.95
MP3 (Audio Book)	$12.95
Kindle	$11.95
PDF Download	$10.95

Hardback *$129 V.E.K. Series - Collector's Edition*

This VEK series is a keepsake collectible and Includes: 1 Autographed Hardback Color copy | 1 Soft Back, |1 CD of the title **Do You Know C.P.R.** ? by Author Victoria E. Kain with Bonus previews.

For all Inquiries or additional orders:

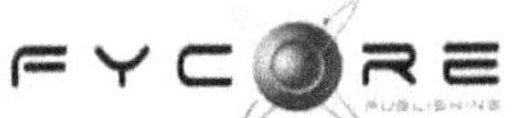

131 Sunset Ave Ste E#353
Suisun City CA, 94585
Office | (800) 470-FYCORE
Facsimile: | (800) 531-0190
Email: | inquiry@fycore.com

Fycore Publishing and Fycore.com are subsidiaries of Gritanium LLC.

ISBN 161910000-2

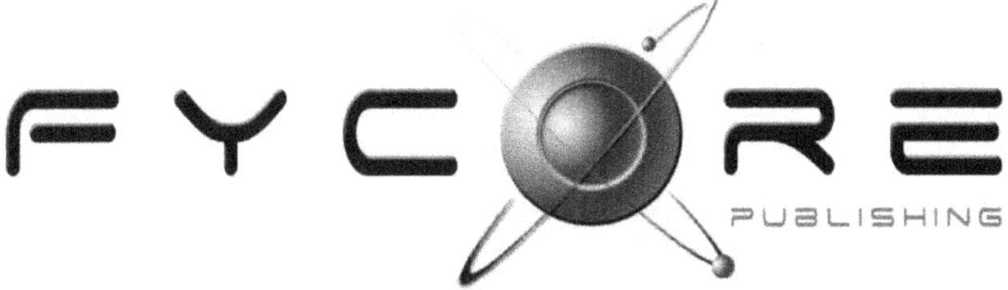

www.fycore.com

Author: **Arnell Lane Hall**
Victoria E. Kain
Illustrations & Graphic Design by: **gritography.com**
Edited by: **Fycore Publishing**
Printing: **Gritanium LLC**

Published August 2011

"DO YOU KNOW C.P.R.?"

Cultivating **P**rofessional **R**elationships

Let's Face It!

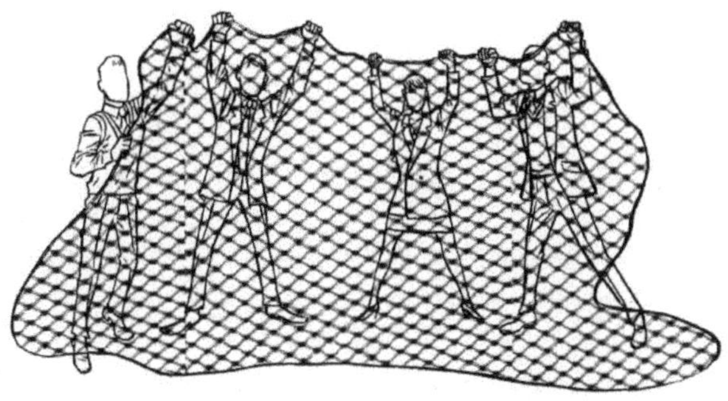

Everything we do in life requires a safety net for support. When we get into our vehicles we immediately buckle up. We are covered up to our necks with life insurance in case of an accident. At the beach there are lifeguards who watch over us in the event of trouble in the water.

With all these support systems we carry around as excess baggage, it is a vivid reminder of our human frailty and the need for support from others. Yet, even knowing that we need support, we often fail to provide a support network for ourselves in the one most critical area of our lives, the "workplace."

Since the workplace is where we spend the most waking hours of our day, it is the one place where we should be protected from the *"what if's"* in life. Find out how cultivating a C.P.R. Network can always help you be at the top of your game from where you stand in "your" workplace!

TABLE OF CONTENTS

Acknowledgments

This book is dedicated to my husband and family for showing patience, love and support during my book writing journey. When I needed to bounce ideas, I bounced them off each of you and was reassured that you were in my corner until my project was complete.

Thank you to my friends who humored me during my book research process. I could not have written these pages without your support. To my publisher who saw my creative side along with the talent I possess, I thank you. Thank you for taking a chance on me and developing my new ideas. Inspiring me to go from telling stories to my siblings on the front porch of my grandparent's home to writing my stories down and now being deemed; "Author."

Also, a special thanks to "Monarch," my "Iron Butterfly." You are the inspiration for all my writings. Your creative genius helps make the things I dream of come true. Your talents are unmatched and untouchable! I thank you all for your endless support in my writing journey and dedicate this first book to you.

Arnell Lane Hall

About the Author

Arnell Lane Hall is a new author that found a passion for writing while sitting on the front porch swing at her grandparent's ranch during summer vacations (see back cover). At the young age of 10, she sat in the old swing on the porch and had her siblings listen while she recited excerpts from what would become manuscripts for her future book ideas.

As an adult, Arnell's father deeded her grandparent's ranch to her wanting her to continue writing, and knew it was part of her inspiration. Arnell aptly calls it "Whispering Pines," because it always gave her a feeling of contentment when she walked amidst the tall pines bordering the family home.

Arnell travelled extensively over the years and found time to acquire multiple degrees in Business, Management, and Psychology. Arnell still finds time to continue what she started as a child, writing her stories on the now refurbished "porch swing" for the "I'll Be Brief" Series!

Arnell Lane Hall

Introduction

An important question we should ask ourselves is: can we survive today's diverse workplace without networking support? If you believe you can, you are sadly mistaken. The "I'll Be Brief" Series of books is written for the 21st century readers and beyond. It is written for those who value the most precious commodity in life, "time." Time is precious because we cannot harness it, we do not own it, so we must not waste it.

One of the main concepts of C.P.R. is to stress the importance of Cultivating Professional Relationships. It is the mainstay for staying relevant in the workplace. It is also the catalyst for ensuring that our books can be read in only one day. When reading our series, we recommend that readers take "time" out of their schedule to relax and refresh their minds with reading that will improve their thinking abilities.

Please note, people who value their time will value the time of others as well. "Do You Know C.P.R.?" takes the straight forward approach to exposing what it takes to cultivate professional relationships in the 21st century workplace.

C.P.R. gives practical scenarios that exist in the workplace and provide answers to real questions that will help guide you in all walks of life.

Whether you are entering the workplace for the first time, changing careers, transitioning from a first retirement or just wanting to sharpen your skills in becoming savvier in the workplace, C.P.R. will work for you! Being adaptable in the workforce today means having the proper tools to navigate from one major point to the next.

Remember, in order to Cultivate Professional Relationships, you must first "plant the seeds." The question for you is: How does your professional garden grow?

Planting the Seeds for Cultivating Professional Relationships

Ah, yes…it's a great day to work in our professional gardens. If you have never planted a garden, you must put it on your things to do list before you expire. Planting seeds is an amazing process, and while we all can appreciate the process of growth, many of us may not understand it. There are several things that must take place when planting "anything!"

Before you can plant seeds, we must first cultivate the ground, or in this case the environment, in which we want the seeds to grow. Since we are referring to figurative gardens in the workplace, we must avail ourselves of establishing new relationships in order to find, or "grow," our C.P.R. prospects. Once we do this, it is the same as planting a seed!

We should always try and keep an open mind in this process which creates a place for C.P.R.'s to share thoughts and ideas with us. This is like watching the seed begin to sprout. Being sincere in our efforts and listening to what others have to say may also open doors to identifying your new C.P.R. prospects.

Once you find those new prospects, remember to always be honest when building the relationships, because these are the "ships" you want to "float" when everything else around you may be sinking. If you already have a C.P.R. network, you need to know what is required to keep it. This can be likened to "watering" or nourishing the relationship.

As previously mentioned, when learning about the areas above, we touched on consulting with others you "trust", which also means you must be "trustworthy." To have ethical people in our C.P.R. network, we must first be ethical ourselves, and practice the adage: "Do unto others as you would have them do unto you."

A simplified way to say this is: If you bring someone a Krispy Creme donut, they will bring you a Starbucks latte or something to that effect. You never want to allow a good deed to go unnoticed or unreciprocated.

It is not the same as buying a friendship or relationship, but it says that you want to share with your new found contacts. Either way, loyalty, trust, respect, honesty, integrity, hard work and fair play are the keys to open any door.

You should always have these on your keychain in the workplace. Remember that the door swings both ways and will close just as quickly if kind gestures are missing from your C.P.R. networking process. It is a fact that professional people will support other professionals inside and outside of the workplace. They do this because they understand that they need the same support from each other and must give it at will in order to get it back when they need it.

It is further understood that when aligning themselves with others, their reputation is on the line. So, when creating your network, never get caught sitting on "deceit". If you do, your network will "unseat" you and consider you damaged goods that will only contaminate the rest of the network.

Our Socioeconomic State is Serious!

"Changing Jobs Today is Crucial, Look Before You Leap."

Is this you? Imagine you are standing before the interviewer for a job you are not sure is right for you. You answered the ad and the basic job description sounds interesting. But you are not sure of the work hours, stress levels of deadlines or benefits package. In order to see the seriousness of valuing our careers or jobs, we must consider our socioeconomic state and the reason we are working in the first place.

There are many things in life that will affect our livelihood. It is a known fact that unemployment and health issues can create a major concern for the wealth of people. Family responsibility can also make a difference in the types of jobs we may choose to accept.

Retirees are now going back to work in order to provide healthcare coverage for themselves and their families. Most of us do not look before we leap into that new job that just happened to say all the right things in the ad we answered. But we should! We may want to think twice about the importance of keeping our jobs regardless of the position we hold. The type of work we perform or how prestigious the position might be is not as important as being able to provide support for ourselves and our family and still have a quality of life to boot.

Today's economic situation dictates that most people will have either a full or part time job with benefits of some sort for survival. At the moment, unemployment is adversely affecting millions of people worldwide. Many countries simply cannot provide their residents with jobs sufficient enough to keep them off the poverty lines. Abraham Maslow's hierarchy of needs is definitely applicable here. We all need core comforts to survive in order to feel balanced.

For this reason, people from other countries will flee to the U.S. or other areas where they can find any kind of work to provide for their families. This, in turn, causes the receiving countries to become hard pressed to support millions of nonresidents with jobs. This creates a shortage of jobs for the residents of that country.

We all should consider how we do what we do in the workplace today and take matters seriously. We need to create a new mindset and a professional network of support for ourselves to eliminate stresses in finding and keeping the right jobs.

One of the most important things people should consider when attempting to find the right job for themselves is to ask: "how connected am I to the people in my workplace?" Since most organizations are moving towards globalization, do we get along with everyone of all nationalities and background? How well do we communicate in person, on the phone or even in writing. Staying connected is the difference between having power for survival at your disposal to stay connected with the people you will be working with.

As mentioned, we spend most of our waking hours at work, so it would stand to reason that we should feel comfortable with those who will be part of our work teams. This concept of pairing the right groups of people together has become so critical that corporations today are very keen on ensuring that when prospective employees are interviewed, they are interviewed with the goal of getting the right personality for the job. The education and resume are only two parts of the process. The goal is to have a sense of connectivity.

Being connected is the only way in many instances today to get and keep the right job for ourselves, because the days are gone where big corporations are solid as a rock.

Today, even the solid rocks are being cut in half and turned to sand that sifts through the many holes in our economic system. We must think about what it takes to stay gainfully employed today and what we need to do in order to be that one person that an employer will seek out to keep, if the sand dwindles down to the bottom of the economic bucket.

Quote

"Money, True Love and Friendship are like the wind; no matter where you find it, you are always blown away."

Arnell Hall

CHAPTER 1
Do You Know C.P.R.?

"Are You Afraid To Ask For Help When You Need It?"

There are times in our lives when we simply fail to ask for the help we know that we need. In some instances we go to sleep at the wheel in our lives and allow our professional situations to fester or grow weeds around it indicating that we have failed to alert anyone that we needed assistance. When this happens, it is an indicator that we have simply given up on ourselves and our professional careers.

Hence the phrase popularized by Queen's Freddy Mercury: ***"Another one bites the dust."***

Once we recognize that we all need support to survive, we will understand why we need to know how to Cultivate Professional Relationships in the workplace. This is why it is likened to the life saving act of C.P.R.

The acronym "C.P.R." is normally interpreted to mean "Cardio Pulmonary Resuscitation." However, in this instance, "C.P.R." is referring to "Cultivating Professional Relationships" and bringing our best to the workplace. Bringing our best affords us the opportunity to create a network of individuals who will support us in a time of need.

In order to do this, you must remember the first tip: any unidentified fish is a shark! Learn it! When you cannot identify an ally, it must be classed as a predator until further notice. The only way you can determine who your allies are is to personally select them over time after testing them out. You might ask: Who can be an ally as for me? The answer is: Anyone in the workplace that is willing to help you navigate through the workforce waters.

Who needs allies? New employees, high school graduates, college graduates, and others are appropriate candidates for the C.P.R. network. How could any of these groups create a C.P.R. network when they do not know who to trust and have not yet established any connections? Remember, C.P.R. is simple, available and practical if you pay attention to your needs in the workplace.

Now that we have discussed allies as part of the process, let's move on to our next phase to see how this actually works. Where can you find these new allies for support, and learn how to be able to identify them as C.P.R.'s? You can find them wherever there are people since they will stand out among the crowd. Once again, C.P.R. is simple, viable and practical and as easy as 1-2-3. Everyone should have a C.P.R. network for survival in the 21st century workplace.

To further our discussion, in finding C.P.R. prospects, always keep an open mind. This creates a place for C.P.R.'s to share thoughts and ideas with you. Being sincere in your efforts and listening to what others have to say may also open doors to identifying your new networkers.

Always be honest in building your relationships because these are the "ships" you will want to "float" when everything else around you may be sinking. If you already have a C.P.R. network, you need to know what is required to keep it. As mentioned previously, when learning about the 1-2-3's above, we touched on consulting with others you "trust" which also means we must be "trustworthy."

To have ethical persons in our C.P.R. network, we must first have ethics and practice the adage: "Do unto others as you would have them do unto you." This is the only way to get and keep your C.P.R. relationships strong so that when tough times are upon you, they will be able to weather the storm. Many people may not understand what this means for their C.P.R. network, but we must remember that in the real world, one hand still washes the other. This further reminds us that whatever others may do to support us, we must remember that we should always find ways to support them as well...and we must be consistent.

A simplified way to say this is: If you bring someone a Krispy Creme donut for the team, then I will bring Starbucks latte's, or something to that effect. Either way, loyalty, trust, respect, honesty, integrity, hard work and fair play are the keys to open any door. Remember, the door swings both ways and will close just as quickly if kind gestures are missing in your C.P.R. networking.

It is a fact that professional people will support other professionals in the workplace. They do this because they want and need the same support you need. Their reputation is on the line when they align themselves with you. So, when creating your network, never get caught sitting on "deceit". If you do, your network will "unseat" you and consider you damaged goods that will only contaminate their network.

Take responsibility for what you do or don't do whether it was right or wrong. Doing so will show that you are willing to accept accountability, and you will be remembered for stepping up to the plate, even if you strike out. Always be ready to take the wheel and drive when it's your turn. Again, it allows others a chance to take a backseat and rest from their labors. It is also a great way to show your willingness to help.

This is where you gain major C.P.R. kudos! By showing your genuine support, you gain the confidence and respect of those you want in your network. When you lend a hand to help on a project, it reinforces your commitment to walk the green mile, as it were. Then everyone will know that you did the right thing. When we learn to develop lasting relationships in the workplace, it is likened to knowing C.P.R. in time of distress.

Remember, you only have one chance to develop the right types of professional relationships. So you must value and protect them when you do. Below are some techniques commonly used. Try them:

1 Anyone with the right skills can assist you.

2 Basic common sense goes a long way with understanding your organization's policy.

3 Reading this book will assist you in achieving the goal of "Cultivating Professional Relationships" throughout your entire career.

With all that is said about C.P.R., there is one serious warning to keep in mind. Beware of the "Negative Ninja's" in the work place, who will cloak their actions and pretend to be in your network. These personality types will do anything to gain the trust of unsuspecting ones and are negative entities and likened to "wolves in sheep clothing" running on negatively charged batteries. Negative Ninja's only want to know where your weaknesses are so they can cripple your C.P.R. network.

You must avoid negativity in the workplace at all cost and always stay positively charged! Your primary goal for reading this book is to learn how to create your C.P.R. network and learn how to protect it. Remember, when forging professional relationships for your network, "Never come to the bargaining table empty handed." But rather, always bring a dish full of "your best efforts."

No one wants to be freeloaded off, but if you need assistance from someone else, be ready to give it in return. Again, professional relationships are based on trust, respect, integrity, loyalty and hard work. Once you are known for these qualities, you will not have to be second guessed by anyone. Other C.P.R.'s will recognize you from a distance and will always welcome you in!

It's time to take a deep breath and go under as we delve deeper into other workplace stresses you may encounter. In order to begin creating a network of support, there are three things you must do in the workplace to stay effective:

Always bring your best efforts; be accessible; Cultivate Professional Relationships. Remember, people who can provide a safety network for us in the workplace will fit all these things mentioned!

When taking on a new job or working to keep your old one, think about what is most important to keeping things stable at work. We must always be a good listener and actually "hear" what is being said. Don't go off half cocked and miss a vital point when you are supposed to be listening for clarifications, instructions and/or directives.

Take time and listen so you will know exactly what is expected of you and how you will deliver the product. Being attentive means more than just sitting and staring at the speaker with a glazed look in your eyes. If you do, everyone knows that you are actually asleep and will have no interest in anything you may have to say now or in the next decade.

Always listen with enthusiasm: not the Barnum and Bailey circus act type of enthusiasm where you continuously nod your head like the car bobbing dolls you see on the dashboards of vehicles.

You want the speaker to know they have your undivided attention. If it is genuine interest, your speaker will know it and will be glad to support any questions you may have at the end. At the first sign of a worker thinking that they are not appreciated, negative stresses begin to form like a dark cloud before a rain storm. If this mindset goes unchecked, some individuals may not get to their first year's performance appraisal.

Understanding Your Work Environment

When coming into an organization, never assume that everything is as it seems. You must find out if the pH is balanced for your survival. An organizational culture is just that: a place where people grow economically, professionally and socially, all at different rates, and times. You must quickly learn what you need to know, since your corporate survival depends on it. Many lose their way on the job early on because they do not adapt to the organizational culture.

The first rule of thumb in the workplace is to avoid any unidentified "fish." They could be predators! If you find that you do not fit in, then stop trying to put the square peg in the round hole. Simply bow out gracefully and move on.

It is crucial in today's job market to get and keep the recognition we need and deserve. Many times, this means taking the assignment that no one else wants. At times this may be allowing a million dollar customer to get on our last nerve in order to close the deal. We must always be ready to do something spectacular to get the attention of those we want in our professional network. When we think of being connected, think of the World Wide Web.

The internet is the only place that anyone can go to and communicate globally in an instant. Being without the World Wide Web for humans is like a spider being unable to spin his web. Without that ability, he is a defenseless insect waiting to become something else's prey.

We are the same without our professional networks. Without others who are connected as well, we do not have the inside support of our organizational figureheads who can affect our positive efforts to stay afloat in this job market.

So, who is in your network? How will you prepare to survive this job crisis? If your job changed today, who would come to your rescue? Have you created any lasting professional relationships that will work for you in the next 2, 5 or 10 years? If not, read on and learn how to stay afloat in these turbulent times! Preparing for and maintaining our employment through the shark infested waters of today's 21st century workplace is truly a must! How serious is the economic situation to you now?

What Does C.P.R. Mean for You In The Workplace?

Sadly, time races by and we begin to feel ourselves sinking under the pressure of the three "P's" in the workplace: Politics, Projects and People. We may feel like a 747 in rush hour traffic on a drastically short runway and no landing gear.

Where our jobs are concerned, we may not even realize we are going under before we can appreciate what a C.P.R. could have done to support our cause and help us keep our employment. Most of us will agree that going under is not an option. So we struggle to stay afloat even though it may cause us to neglect our families, health and jobs. Many may think that giving less on the job will relieve stress. But when our jobs are neglected, this creates more stresses for us. Let's discuss how!

When our jobs become stressful and we feel we can't go on, some feel they can slack off doing their work to the best of their ability. They may rationalize that they have done a good job for a long time and it's okay to "relax" a bit! Not!!! Once our work life force begins to be drained out of us, others trying to save themselves will come running like sharks to a feeding frenzy. They will be ready to feed on the potential opportunities that may surface in the event of our demise. At this point we know that we are in trouble!

This process is called Darwinian workforce "survival of the fittest." At this point, we need to know who our C.P.R's are in the workplace. It is the only way we can stay afloat the right way. Knowing a C.P.R. gives you access to instant confidential mentoring and counseling. When we need to vent, we need to know who we can vent to and not be judged incorrectly. Staying afloat may sometimes mean changing careers.

If this happens, don't panic! Change is not always a bad thing if what you are GOING to do is less stressful than what you are currently doing. Some in your C.P.R. network may be able to advise you on matters of changing careers or shifting responsibilities that fit your skill set and needs. You need to know the best course of action for you at that time so that you make the right decisions that will benefit your future. Having this network will help you stay clear of the pitfalls that reside in all workplaces.

Now you can take a deep breath and get ready to dive in and see how you can create a C.P.R. network to avoid ending up as shark bait with no hope of ever being resuscitated, or worse...taking your work home with you!

Quote:

"Success is not determined by whether I can count on Me, Myself and I, but whether after I succeed, if I.O.U."

– Victoria E. Kain

CHAPTER 2
Know the Signs of Workplace Distress

" Are you concerned about why your stress levels are so high?"

Are You In Too Deep?

Sometimes we can be so deeply involved in what ails us that we miss the obvious issues that are causing the problem. Now it's time to recap what we've covered so far! We have discussed our economic state, planting the seeds, understanding your workplace and what C.P.R. means for you in the workplace. Now let's take a look at Scenario 1 involving M.I. Mediocre, a seemingly good career that goes "SOUTH." This is a situation where the individual ignored all the signs that led up to their demise. However, read it and weep and see if you can identify any pitfalls and stresses M.I. Mediocre overlooked."

Gulp…gulp…

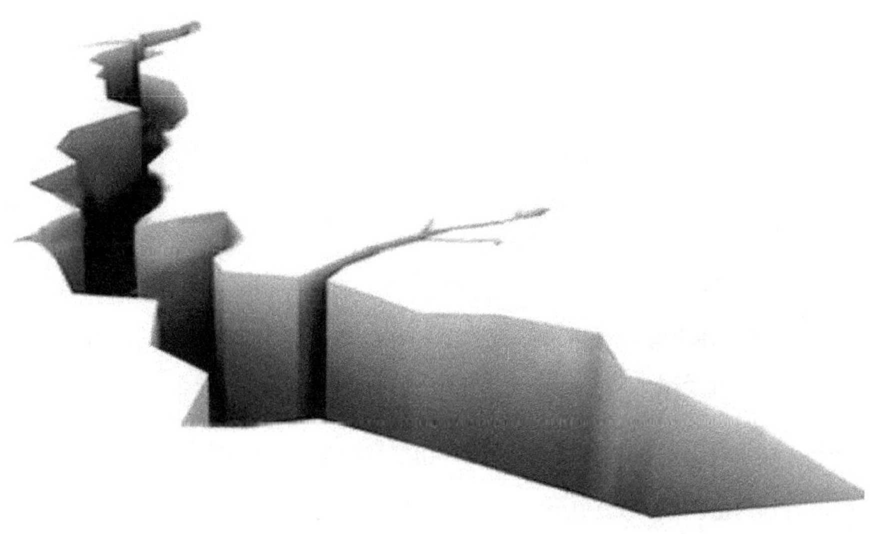

SCENARIO I - M.I. Mediocre?

M.I. Mediocre is an average worker who does just enough to get by. They manage a department of 35 employees, all having diverse backgrounds. M. I. Mediocre has been a manager for several years. The last two years they managed to escape company downsizing using seniority. During the third quarter, Mediocre missed 3 project deadlines, and failed to report the results of their department efforts when the boss needed to see the numbers. Mediocre had many other personal and professional distractions and felt justified in their neglect.

M.I. Mediocre likes everyone, for the most part, but today, are racking their brain trying to see why they are called for an unannounced meeting with the vice president. Mediocre quickly remembers, "ah, yes...it's bonus time," and shrugs any other reason that they could be invited to this meeting.

Even though Mediocre is satisfied with the thought of this discussion being about a bonus, today is the first time forethought was given to their career as well. They chose to look at the bright side, which is always a good thing, "they thought." This meeting could be nothing but good! So they thought.

Unknown to Mediocre, a few employees in their department wanted to leave because of their poor leadership style and one dimensional attitude. Most of the employees never left the department due to the economic state and needing the job. M.I. Mediocre had sadly chalked it up to the employees wanting to stay in their department.

M.I. also showed biased tendencies. They looked down on those under them and rarely smiled, but never said anything positive or upbuilding to anyone except their personal friends. In fact, at times, M.I. Mediocre was simply rude! M.I. Mediocre is content with their job and if they don't get the bonus or raise, they can live with it. Mediocre cannot think of any reason why they would be denied a bonus or raise. Mediocre was always hard pressed to admit their wrongdoing but then again, they never did any wrong or needed to apologize if they were wrong.

As Mediocre walked to the conference room, they made a concerted effort to smile as they passed by the other office managers who gave a quick glance and returned the smile. Mediocre approaches the conference room door and hesitates for a moment in order to gain their composure before entering.

Mediocre finally opened the door and enters the room. The Senior Manager is there and is smiling and thanks Mediocre for coming. There was a sick feeling in the pit of their stomach because the vice president is not there and they feel they may not get the raise they deserve. Mediocre is not at ease and begins to feel apprehensive. The Senior Manager sits at the desk and picks up a file in one hand. They commence to hand Mediocre a copy and then pick up coffee and drink it.

Mediocre does the same and retrieves a cup as well. The Senior Manager begins explaining why Mediocre is there and as they talk, Mediocre gets a text and answers it briefly. Mediocre sadly excuses the interruption and the Senior Manager continues. Mediocre can't help but focus on the many justifications for the big bonus they are anticipating. As the Senior Manager is halfway finished with what they are saying, their last words are: "You are being fired as of this date."

They then ask Mediocre if there are any questions and then Mediocre, still not paying attention states: "Can you repeat that, please?" Pause. "I did not catch that." The Senior Manager repeats it, and Mediocre is stunned!

Mediocre has just been fired from the company. They were thanked for their efforts but shown where they did not meet the mark of what the expectations were to continue in their current role. Sticker shocked back to reality, Mediocre is in disbelief and moves mechanically as they leave the building. On the way down from the 15th floor, Mediocre tries to think positively, but nothing seems to surface. As Mediocre steps out of the elevator and is a good distance away to the parking lot, Mediocre turns and looks at the place where they had been employed for many years.

It was as if they were looking at a burning building in disbelief. Mediocre finally begins to realize many of the things they had NOT done to secure their job. The bad attitude with the employees, their unwillingness to cooperate with their peers or meeting set deadlines mandated by their superiors, along with practicing good time management and caring for their direct reports each day became obvious and glaring mistakes. Mediocre also now realized there was no one there to speak positively in their behalf at their last day on the job. In short, Mediocre just wasn't cutting it.

There were no lasting good work habits that captured anyone's attention which limited their ability to cultivate professional relationships with those who may have helped them stay relevant in the workplace.

Would M.I. Mediocre have fared better if they had cultivated a better work ethic? Would they have fared better with a C.P.R. network? Could they have discussed any of their issues beforehand to avoid being fired? This is the smoking gun affect!

Let's dive into our next topic of workplace warning signs.

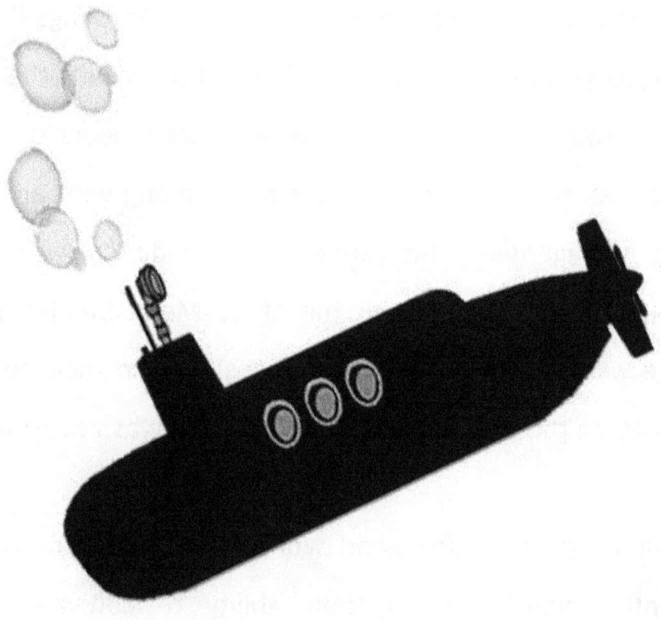

Don't Ignore Workplace Warning Signs!

There are many people worldwide experiencing the M.I. Mediocre scenario. This is why it is essential to cultivate professional relationships and habits inside and outside of the workplace. With jobs becoming more difficult to find and keep, any issues can be overwhelming, especially issues you can't control. Remember, always give your best to the company you work for regardless of what you do for a living.

Also remember that bad attitudes and negative relationships in the workplace are never acceptable. Remember when you work for a Company, they are paying you for your BEST efforts. Anything less than your best can be deemed theft of the company's time and resources, and we all know these two things are valuable commodities.

Always cultivate professional relationships so that you can be supported if decisions are made that could affect your employment. Now ask yourself if you are experiencing anything similar to what M.I. Mediocre experienced? If so, do you see any areas in your job performance or history that would put you at risk for missing a promotion or raise, or heavens forbid, an untimely job change?

No one has ever gotten fired, demoted, overlooked, passed over, or transferred without there being some forethought, conversation, documentation, or collaborating in the process. The word "fired" is an action word. It takes effort, energy, paperwork and collaboration to achieve. Companies typically look for the positive things a valued employee does, even if they fall behind in meeting the standards from time to time.

Being proactive and identifying any signs early on yourself, and making corrections or recommendations to your Manager for support will save you the financial trouble and humiliation of being let go if these vital things go unchecked.

However, in the unfortunate event that you are fired, take what you have learned and correct the problems that caused you to lose your job in the first place. Then, become a better employee in the next company to erase the negative record. Take a quick look back at M.I. Mediocre and see if there were things that they could have done to avoid being fired. List five things you found in their scenario.

Then, answer the questions yourself and see if, in your own job situation, there are things you may be overlooking that could be hot spots to consider addressing immediately. See how well you fare!

M.I. Mediocre was actually fired for a number of reasons they failed to recognize beforehand. Yes, poor performance on any level at work will never be tolerated. Poor performance will always jeopardize employment at some point. In scenario 1, Mediocre should have known that lack of performance and negative attitude displayed in working with others is unacceptable.

LIST 5 THINGS M.I. MEDIOCRE IGNORED AT WORK

1 ____

2 ____

3 ____

4 ____

5 ____

Sometimes, it is easier for us to see the mistakes of others before we can see our own. This is one of the main reasons we ask the readers to list what they considered to be the 5 main things M.I. Mediocre missed. Although there were many, when you list the ones that were obvious to you, you may want to consider why those particular ones stood out in your mind. It may be that you will find some of those same shortcomings in your own list. You may begin your list.

LIST 5 THINGS ON YOUR JOB YOU MAY BE IGNORING

1 ____

2 ____

3 ____

4 ____

5 ____

Now that you have completed your list of things you feel are missing in your workplace, you must review this list carefully because it could be the same list that is used in the unfortunate event your services are no longer needed in your organization. The key is to CORRECT your list NOW! If the first item included in your list is related to missing deadlines, you should immediately consider "Time Management" courses or refreshers. There are also online training guides that can help you become successful in meeting your deadlines. Once you have corrected these 5 things, you may be on your way to becoming that employee that employers will seek out. The key is to "BEGIN NOW, and to CONTINUE the positive actions."

CHAPTER 3

The Signs That Lead Up To Being Fired

"Have you lost your workplace initiative?"

Ready - Aim - Fired!

O.k., you just got sacked! Depending on how it happened, you may be somewhat devastated but not traumatized. First, remember that, although it is an unfortunate occurrence, people get fired every day. So we should keep a level head if it should happen to us. No one wants this to happen, but in today's job market, none of us want to be on the other end of a firing squad. It is a fact of life as we know it, and especially in our era.

If you have not cultivated any professional relationships in your past, we may have to start searching for the needle in the haystack. If you have cultivated professional relationships, help may be as close as a phone call away from your being gainfully employed in a short while. Take action before the lack of employment takes a toll on your livelihood.

Having this C.P.R. network is likened to being in the ocean in trouble and someone performs C.P.R. to resuscitate you back to life. Without C.P.R.'s, the longer you stay under in the cold corporate waters after you have been sacked, the harder it is to be resuscitated. The key is to recover fast.

Time is of the essence and survival is the key. Knowing the signs of a firing coming on is crucial to your long term survival. We saw how Mediocre allowed themselves to be slam dunked like a Magic Johnson nightmare rerun. No one should ever be that blindsided if they have ANY form of vision. Now that we see what could have been avoided and why, let's look at Scenario II and see how the outcome can be different when you see a job situation about to change...

You have done everything right on the job, and you have professional relationships in the workplace working for you. Haven't we seen this many times in the movies where some big shot was being asked to step down from their prominent position? The term "stepping down" is just a politically correct way to say "you're fired," while the camera is still on you. Let's Roll 'em! Action!

SCENARIO II - R.U. Topnotch?

R.U. Topnotch, a corporate manager, is asked to meet the Vice President of the company for lunch at the country club. Topnotch has always had a good relationship with the vice President and many others in the company. On their way to lunch Topnotch recants in their mind how the company's budget is dwindling. They remembered they have always worked and supported their team and others in the company.

On many occasions T. Notch supported special community venues that they enjoyed being involved in and took time out of their own schedule to support a cause to benefit others. People always appreciated the support. This meeting with the vice president is nothing different for T. Notch and there is no fear because their work record is impeccable.

T. Notch arrives at the restaurant and greets the President with a smile and a handshake as usual. The vice President and T. Notch laugh, and share a great healthy lunch. T. Notch and the vice president begin to talk about the down side of the business and T. Notch's department. They discuss an economic issue with the company and the need to downsize.

T. Notch takes a sip of their coffee and raises an eyebrow and says, "Well", I do understand that things are getting a bit tight in the company's budget. T. Notch gently places their napkin on the table. The president then says, "T. Notch," you've had some good years with the company. I'll make some phone calls for you.

T. Notch, picks up the cup of coffee and finishes it. Then T. Notch states, "I understand." They thank the vice president for the opportunity to have worked with such a great team. Lunch was over. What just happened? T. Notch just lost their job. This is where C.P.R. comes in: The vice president then states, In the meantime T. Notch, take a couple of weeks off with your family. Just like that, lunch is over.

T. Notch was just "let go". How could that be? There were no tears or swearing about how they had worked their proverbial buttocks off for nothing. There was also no name calling or slandering others who they may have thought deserved to be let go instead of them and their department. Instead, in this scenario, there was a professional relationship already intact to quickly resuscitate T. Notch back to his original state of employment.

The president respected Notch by giving them the courtesy to deliver the news personally. The vice president knew that Notch was a loyal team player and recommended them to another company for employment. Something as simple as a phone call in a distressful work situation such as this can be likened to a life ring being thrown to you in the middle of the ocean. There was no shark frenzy here with Top Notch. They were supported by their C.P.R. Network. Smooth sailing!

Recap. T. Notch's scenario was much better than Mediocre's. T. Notch had their C.P.R. network in place and it served them well! If you want to be successful in the workplace, you must understand how to create your own C.P.R. network so it can work to keep you "working."

You must do everything in your power to avoid being fired from your job, even if it means taking extra time out to support others around you before it happens. You never know where your personal "life saver" may come into focus.

All employees must have a plan to avoid losing their job in this recovering economy today. As for many situations, like the above scenario, there are numerous guides to preventing job loss, as it depends on the culture and environment you work in.

All who fail to plan will usually fail, unless they take the necessary steps to keep from losing their jobs or occupation. Employees today must insure that their work place is free from potential job hazards. This means putting solutions in place before a firing takes place. Remember, only you can prevent a work place firing!

IDENTIFY 5 POSITIVE THINGS THAT TOP NOTCH DID

1 ______________________________

2 ______________________________

3 ______________________________

4 ______________________________

5 ______________________________

In this scenario 2, it was obvious that R.U. Topnotch was at the top of their game. There were no true surprises in this scenario. They were up to speed on what was happening not only in their department, but had looked at the bigger picture and ensured that they were abreast of the company's economic stance. They showed no fear of being let go, and was able to get the golden parachute as it were after lunch was over. This is how it should be for those who have a C.P.R. network. It is the culmination of having cultivated the right seeds in the right soil at the right time!

LIST 5 THINGS THAT TOP NOTCH DID NOT IGNORE AT WORK

1 ______________________________

2 ______________________________

3 ______________________________

4 ______________________________

5 ______________________________

T. Notch did not ignore **"ANYTHING"** on their job. This indicated they were well trained, had listened and paid attention to everything they heard and visualized. Now when it was time to harvest, or utilize some of their professional "yield," they actually had something to reap from those professional relationships that had been forged months or years earlier. When you know you have given your best to your employer, there is no fear or dread of the "what if's" in the work place!

Things that contribute to being "fired" must include:

- Make sure you read and understand the company's policy. They call it "policy" for a reason. It should be "handy" if you are not sure of something you want or need to know.

- Know your superiors and the things that are unacceptable to them. If you know they are dieting then don't make fat jokes, "ANYWHERE" in the building. Use discernment.

- Pay attention to actions and attitudes in your work environment that could be flammable.

- The old adage that the "customer" is always right is still in effect today: use it!

- Never skimp on your responsibilities in the workplace. When you slack off at work, you leave yourself vulnerable to creating bad work habits.

- Not understanding your work environment creates unnecessary stress and frustration, along with inability to achieve the stated results.

- Be willing to ask for help.
- Consult with your superiors when you smell smoke in the workplace. Always be ready to press the alarm button (per se) when you need help.

And remember...only you can prevent "workplace" firings!

If You Get Fired, Get Fired Up!

Sometimes, even when we do our best we may still lose our job for reasons beyond our control. In this instance, if you get fired, "get fired up"! Don't automatically assume that you have no options at all if you lose your employment. Being fired is never easy to accept, but if it should happen, be prepared by having some place to turn to. The first thing you don't want to do if you lose your job is, "lose your control." Always stay calm in a situation such as this in order to clearly think through the options you may have.

Most people do not feel as energetic in a situation such as this and having a copy of your resume on hand will get you moving on the job search very quickly. Always keep an updated resume in your possession. This will save you time and energy if you should lose your employment. If you already have a degree, search for the type of jobs that will get you employed quickly in areas you are interested in or areas you would like to work in.

Sometimes people who have lost their job look for only one type of job. The key is to be reemployed quickly to keep your income stable. Even if you find a job, and do not particularly like it, it does not mean you must keep it forever.

This thought process is geared to help the person who has lost their source of income get back to work quickly. Remember, you can still apply for the jobs you truly want while you are employed. The key here is to stay "active." Also remember, it is better to be employed when applying for another job. It also makes salary negotiations better as well. If you lose your job and are awarded unemployment benefits, apply for it immediately. Should you begin work before your benefits start, you can remove the request. **This is very important.** The next thing is; if you do not find a job within the first 30-60 days, look for fresh new jobs in other areas that you can work. The key is to be actively "Working!"

Quote:

"Good relationships should always stay afloat…Never allow them to wash up on shore."

– Louisa Casborn

CHAPTER 4

When to Know and Tell

"Information is Power."

Information is Power...Harness it!

Even if you know who to trust or not to trust, some information should be guarded. Information has always been man's most viable power resource. Sharing information is our way of communicating thoughts and ideas. With it, many things have taken place, both bad and good, in our society.

As we have discussed in the previous chapters, there are some in the workplace who may sabotage your career. If you are not cautious, you could become a victim of saboteurs. As mentioned, saboteurs need information to fuel their agendas. They can't get started until you give them the gas they need in the form of information.

The only way anyone can get information is if you give it to them. For this reason, it is important to know when to speak and when to keep quiet. A rule of thumb: You speak about things when you need to, otherwise, it is someone else's business and you should stay out of it. However, if you know something that could help someone, you may choose to speak about this to the proper personnel. "Knowledge is said to be power, only if you use it correctly."

Today's employers must know that you know that you know! There is no substitute or excuse for not knowing your job. If you know it well, you want to share what you know with others. Instead of spreading knowledge to those who would use it unwisely try mentoring or volunteering to present your knowledge at community venues or speeches. This will be a viable way to share your knowledge with those who can truly appreciate it.

Now that you are in the "know", focus on the advantages of what you know and how it will assist you in your quest to succeed. Remember: Don't step on those in your path as you go up the corporate ladder, as you will surely see them again if you find yourself coming back down. Information will cause you to be better than the competition, all things being equal. However, you must always be in the information gathering mindset.

Ambition and initiative will normally dictate how far you must climb to reach the top of the corporate ladder. Remember, as you go up or down the ladder, two "rungs" don't make a right. Know where your heart is and shoot for the moon! If you miss it, shoot again and this time aim a little higher to hit your target.

Using your knowledge and research as a source of inspiration to get the job you want or keep the one you have is the only way to survive.

Only you can cancel out information "noise" and began to grow from it. Other ways to determine if you tell too much of what you know is to ask yourself these questions.

- Do people at work know your life history after a day or two on the job?

- Can someone that works on the 5th floor come to you on the 1st floor and ask how your Aunt Ell is if they have never met you before?

- Can the maintenance man see you in the hallway and thank you for the invitation to your son's graduation?

If you can say "yes" to any of these questions you are giving out TOO MUCH INFORMATION! Remember, there should always be things you know that your own mother doesn't know about you, let alone people in the workplace who are total strangers.

Sadly though, many of our intimate secrets are divulged at work with the intent of appearing to have nothing to hide, even though some things should be kept undisclosed or only divulged on a need to know basis.

By keeping things that are personal and private, "personal and private", you never have to fear your vital information being spread like peanut butter on compromised bread. It just doesn't hold up. If you are single, do not talk about your break up with a friend, boy or girl, over lunch or the water cooler.

For heaven's sake, do not talk about intimate or personal details on your cell phone in a crowded room, the rest rooms, or other public places. People do not really want to hear all the drama in our lives and besides, most companies forbid the use of such electronic devices in the workplace because of the breach of confidential information that can be picked up through a "blue tooth".

Some companies are installing blocking devices for cell phones at work for emergency calls only during work hours using the same policy that medical offices use. This is primarily because people are clogging the airwaves and scrambling signals that pace-maker patients need to survive with cell phone jargon.

If you are married, do not talk about your husband's smelly gym socks or expose that he chews tobacco! Ewwww! Be a little aloof at least the first 30 days on a new job. Have the military mindset and only give your name, rank, and serial number, as if you have been caught behind enemy lines until you know with whom you are speaking.

This doesn't mean that you should not communicate with others in the workplace. But rather, when you talk, discuss those basic things that are universal and appropriate to talk about, e.g., your kids games, bowling or even bake sales. Have a sense of mystery about your personal or private life, unless there is a need to know. But do not appear to be suspicious.

With all that said, how do you know when to tell something that has been told to you? Even if you have already heard it from one source and are asked by another, "Did you know that?" You should always respond to those types of open ended questions with, "Know what, is this something I need to know?" Or, if it is something that you do need to know, you can simply state, "No, what?" Basically you're asking them to tell you what you need to know. Otherwise "play dumb" in order to allude the gossip syndrome at work.

Always ask yourself this question before you accept information from others at work. "What is knowing this information going to cost me?" Conversely, a question of equal importance to ask is: What is telling this information going to cost me?

Too many times we are in situations where we don't know who and how many people are "swimming in muddy waters." So, if there are workplace indiscretions going on, steer clear of any idle gossip because you do not want your name associated with anything that is being spread whether it is true or false. Some information you know may affect individuals all the way up the corporate chain of a company. You don't want to be swimming in those waters when something hits the top. Most people end up losing their shirt, socks and sometimes shoes. Remember, once words leave our mouths they can come back and the damage is done. So don't get involved in telling or receiving idle gossip, or you will become guilty by association... Now it is time to dive..dive...dive...and take cover!

Quote

"Voodoo Economics",

the only way to balance a

checkbook in the 21st Century.

– Victoria E. Kain

CHAPTER 5
Trust is a Must To Survive In The Workplace

"Do You Know Who To Trust In A Time of Need?"

Learn Who To Trust In The Workplace

Now that you know the power of information, who can you trust in the workplace to share information with? Do you remember the first rule of trust from Chapter 1? If you cannot identify who your allies are, remember that any unidentified fish is a "SHARK," and therefore is a predator.

If you remember this first rule, you're off to a good start. Even though you know this rule, you still have to learn who you CAN trust. During our many and varied lifespans, we must trust many people. As infants we trust our parents or care givers. We trust our teachers and coaches. We trust our family and close friends.

At work, we trust our "instincts!" We have to trust somebody or you will get absolutely "NOWHERE" in life. In our daily lives we must show that we have a measure of trust in others. When the mailman brings your mail, you TRUST that he is who he appears to represent so you take the mail. In order to survive, learn to recognize those who are trustworthy. You trust your physician and tell him your intimate secrets, whether he relishes hearing them or not. We trust these people because they are in their professions as service providers, and we have been conditioned to identify who they are and what they can do to benefit us.

In the workplace there is no difference. We must learn who we can and cannot trust. Think for a moment about M.I. Mediocre. They were reluctant to meet with the Senior Manager, yet R.U. Top Notch was not concerned at all and welcomed the invitation because they had trust in this person.

Now that you know the power of information, who can you trust in the workplace? If you remember the first rule of trust, it states; if you cannot identify who your allies are, consider them a predator. If you always keep this rule in mind, you are off to a good start. Even though you know this rule, you still have to learn who you CAN trust. In life, you have to trust somebody or you will get absolutely "NOWHERE!"

In our lives, we find individuals in the workplace that we may learn to trust, as R.U. Topnotch did, and it served him well. Trust is something that is earned so always ensure that the people you put your trust in have actually earned it. We trust many people every day and do not give it a second thought. Our mailman, our physician, our dentist, our barber, our parents...and the list can go on. We never expect these individuals to do anything that would cause us not to trust them, and most of them are good examples of the roles they are in.

Never Put All Of Your Eggs In One Omelet

The difference between the two scenarios is that M.I. Mediocre had not developed a professional relationship with anyone and Top Notch had. M.I. Mediocre may have been able to reduce the threat of the firing to a warning notice if major things had not been ignored. This alternate approach would have given them time to realize what was about to happen. Also, they may have had the choice to leave on their own and reduce the unnecessary stresses caused by being fired.

Knowing who to trust at work is very important to creating a secure network for survival. Some of you may be wondering, "What about those who try to undermine your work ethic on the job"? Well, you must find out what their agenda is first before you put your full trust in them. Remember, as aforementioned there are many people who are friendly with everyone and simply mean you no harm.

Every office has a Miz. Biscuits, the baker who bakes goodies and leaves them all over the lunch room every week. Now, Miz. Biscuits could care less who the Negative Ninjas are in the workplace because in their mind they are up to their eyebrows in dough each night to supply the comfort food for the staff the next day.

They will feed the ninja's right along with everyone else. Even the negative ninja's will not sabotage Miz. Biscuits because they like being fed too! Also, the Negative Ninjas will not sabotage Miz. Biscuits because that would be the same as going rabbit hunting with a Gatlin gun...it is OVER KILL! Fur and paws everywhere, and after it's all said and done, you will still have nothing to hang your teeth on afterwards. You can trust the Miz. Biscuits, the bakers of the workplace.

There is also another "go to" person who will sympathize with you on anything. This can be another person who you can trust...we will call them, Joe Handy or (Jandy for short). Jandy comes in early and stays late. They know something about everything. They are not your typical promotion hogs and are not looking for the big prominent position and will always support the team.

You can trust them because whenever you need something, the Jandy's of the workplace will always come in handy. These are just a few personality types that you CAN trust. What you want to beware of are those who thrive on a lack of honesty, integrity and trust.

Remember that workplace saboteurs are always scouting the workplace for new bait. They are setting up the nets so that later on they can have full control and feed regularly on the negativity that exist in the workplace.

Once you identify these "shark" like personalities, you must move away from them quickly. Your actions need to counteract theirs. But never tip them off that you are on to them or they will go under and you will never see that side of them again. Then they will surface later with a whole new identity that you may not recognize.

Ask yourself these ten questions that could begin identifying negativity in the workplace. Anyone you suspect of being a Negative Ninja, run them through this list, even if they come up clean.

1. Are people afraid of them?

When people show fear of others at work, this could indicate many things. One thing it could indicate is a controlling person. People who want to be in control may dominate others they feel are weak. When people are timid, they tend not to create any dust when it comes to doing what they are told to do regardless of who is doing the telling.

2. Do they accept feedback from anyone?

They never want feedback. It is the same as getting reverb from a microphone when it is too close to the amplifier.

3. Do they do ANYTHING to get to the top?

Doing anything to get to the top is another area of the person who wants to dominate others. Those who want to rise quickly like popping fresh dough, will not only try to bully their way up the ladder but will step on, climb over, pole vault or even shimmy to get to the next place.

4. Is EVERYTHING always about them?

Everything is always about them. If something is not done their way, you and everyone else will hear about it.

5. Do they have a clue as to the company's Mission?

The company's mission to most of the Negative Ninja's is mission "IMPOSSIBLE." They consider the company's mission as something that only affects the people that are above them and since they are trying to get to that level, they do not worry themselves with it.

6. Do they constantly complain about "EVERYBODY"?

For Negative Ninja's, complaints are an everyday thing. The more people they work with, the larger their pool of complaints will be. Most Negative Ninja's appear to be narcissistic and always want the attention on them, especially if there is someone important around. They will complain long and loud when they do not want others to be in the limelight.

7. Do they get mad if given more work?

When more work is even eluded to, both of their fingers are pointing to someone else. Most Negative Ninja's do not want to take on extra tasks. To them, they have bigger fish to fry and the oil is hot and ready.

8. Do they do good work?

Usually their work is shoddy, but camouflaged. They will always try to talk a good game but will never be able to back it up if pressed for data.

9. Are they sought out by the boss or shunned?

Usually Negative Ninja's are not openly sought after for special projects unless they have not been exposed. In this instance, they may be asked to do some things and will stand on the backs of others in order to get the recognition. If they should succeed in fooling the right folks, they will only hire those like themselves because they never want to be upstaged.

10. Does everyone in the office know their personal problems?

Yes, most Negative Ninja's will tell their personal business in order to gain the sympathies of others. It also is a very crafty ploy to draw those unsuspecting ones into their lair in order to prey on them for a later feeding. The fact is that these relationships are void of life. They are shallow to say the least.

Quote

"Cultivating relationships is an art: it only takes the right attitude and a vivid imagination to paint the most beautiful picture of yourself and share it with everyone you meet."

– Victoria E. Kain

CHAPTER 6
Identifying Negative Ninja's At Work

"Does Negativity have you on the run in the workplace?"

Negativity In The Workplace

Now that you have considered what C.P.R is and how to plant the seeds for creating this network, you must understand and immediately recognize how to guard yourself from being undermined by workplace distresses and sabotage tactics. We remember that information is power but only to the one flipping the switch. So stay in the know!

If you get fired, GET fired up and learn techniques to keep you employed. Now we will talk about some of the hidden agendas of those in the workplace we will call Negative Ninjas. You meet them in and outside the workplace. The aforementioned information will help you to avoid exposing all of your knowledge to those who may not have your best interest at heart.

Don't be alarmed if you are not able to identify the hidden agendas of most people at work during your first encounter. Initially, you must try to seek them out to see if they will fit in your network. It will take some time and effort. Remember that all agendas are not bad, and some are concealed for business reasons. However, you should not be shocked when you find out what some of the agendas are.

It will take some practice, but always remember that there is a hidden agenda in every office and cube in the workplace. You must become better equipped to navigate through these and uncover the hidden agendas that could benefit or harm your career. Doing so will prevent you from "becoming" the next agenda in a negative way.

The pitfalls in the workplace agenda could contribute to political mayhem, that is so deep that you will need special gear to wade through it. What if you have already taken the plunge in your new workplace and you are faced with this dilemma of a negative agenda? Now what? Well, you need to figure out how you can equip yourself to handle everything that you will be exposed to in acquiring this new information.

Remember the 60-90 day rule. In the first 60 days on any job, you should ask, inquire, query or just straight out "pry" for all the information you think you will need to know for the future. The reason you must ask early on is because people are friendlier and more willing to give you the scoop, statistics, air dirty laundry, buy you lunch, brunch and even candy bars within this time frame with no thought of an expectation behind it. It is expected that in the first sixty days on the job you are "learning!!!"

They consider it a courtesy and an honor to tell you (the NEWBIE) everything you need to know because they feel that you don't know anyone to go back to and tell anything you've learned, especially if its personal.

People like feeling as if they have given the new guy the proverbial "scoop." They also believe you will forget it, like most people do, when they walk away because of cramming so much information into a short amount of time. At this time, you can liken yourself to a human sponge! You must suck up all information and store it in your "Broca", the part of the brain that is known to control speech. At some point you may have to remember what you have seen and you may need to share it with others.

Beware! After 90 days, if you asked the same questions, heads will spin, eyebrows will be raised, people will start talking and wondering if you know too much and are setting up your own agenda of who's who for the "what if's" down the road. Always remember, that the Negativity Ninjas know that you know what they know. So, what about those workplace Ninja's that live to spread negativity about you and others in the workplace? An open spot gives them a great vantage point to support the team by picking up the slack you have left behind by your untimely departure that they may have underhandedly supported.

Getting ahead on the job, to some people, may mean whirling a 40 inch machete at the vicinity of some unsuspecting worker's neck, and lopping it off at their desk on their lunch hour. It may not be as drastic as that, but for the sake of this book, we want to ensure that you understand the seriousness of going to sleep at the workplace wheel. There are many things that people learn when they begin a new job. The best time to learn it is BEFORE you get the job! One thing you need to know is who is in your environment. Who are the allies? Who are the Negative Ninjas?

This part is intense because it attempts to identify the undermining acts of some of those in today's workplace. We need to know that these types of personalities exist in order to maintain our stress balance in the workplace. If you are in a new work environment, you are not in tune to your environment enough to assume anything.... So DON'T! Getting to know the teams you will work with will take some time. So do yourself a huge favor and take the time needed to bring others in close to you.

Remember that each person is different and will require different levels of communication. So do not overload or underload anyone from the beginning with information. You must allow people an opportunity to get to know you.

Over time, you will automatically know who your allies will be because you will determine who they are based on the professional relationship you develop with them over time.

Once you have determined who your allies are, they will move into another level of the relationship with you. When this happens, you will be able to differentiate between the C.P.R.'s actions and the Negative Ninjas. Guard your professional reputation and relationship against the negative personality types and cling to the positive types. Negative Ninjas feed on the easy prey. Those who are willing to take excessive risks by divulging too much information too soon could become prey to those who do not have your best interest at heart.

Most Negative Ninjas don't want their actions noticed, so they hide who they really are and use any information they have received for their own benefit. They may pretend to show a positive exterior for the entire world to see, and dupe the world into judging them from their outward appearance. These negative personality types look for power in the information they receive from others which makes them feel invincible.

They move swiftly and quietly through the offices and cubes of departments, even befriending maintenance personnel for vital information. Negative Ninjas do not function on their own power because these personality types are usually narcissistic and tend to think a lot of themselves and do not give to others in a large way. Their goal is to discredit other's positive efforts that may get noticed by the boss. Therefore, the only way to discredit a Top Notcher, is to destroy their credibility in the workplace.

A Negative Ninja wants to gain power at any price. Remember that information is power. So guard specific information that should not be shared with those who have no need for it. This is how you must view Negative Ninjas in order to understand their make up and be able to counteract their attacks on your character.

This can be done without succumbing to their plea for acceptance which is designed to draw you in for the ultimate sacrifice. Remember that some of the stressors we see on the job are self-induced and can be avoided. Giving too much information could cause us issues with others knowing too much about our personal lives or professional goals when they are not in a position to effect them.

Even though Negative Ninjas exist in the workplace, they have to survive too. The only way to disarm the Negative Ninjas is to share only positive information with them which does not fuel their negativity quest to spread idle gossip.

In turn, they will be forced to go elsewhere to spread their negativity and thereby leaving you to continue performing at the highest level for your employer and team.

This is one simple way to disarm the Negative Ninjas and they are "Disarmed." Often times the workplace may appear cold with the changing times. It may seem that there are no more nice guys per se that we can readily see for support. We all need to cut to the chase and recognize what we see and know how to deal with it if we want to survive.

Some of the things you have read in this book you may already know. Some things you may have experienced and did not realize what you were dealing with. Now, that was not so bad was it? You will be able to do some of the things suggested in this book in order to swim in the waves with the "big fish" and feast from their table without being gutted for shark bait.

With these suggestions, you are able to identify when there is turbulence in the workplace waters and know what streams are off limits and when it is time to veer off and go under until the turbulence subsides. Now you are able to stay float and can swim alongside the big fish!

Quote

"Respect is like a paycheck:

You have to earn it."

– Kerry Hall.

CHAPTER 7
Know Your Never's

" Never Burn Both Ends of The Candle. "

Things You Never Do At Work

Now you have an idea of what to do... here is what you should know. In order to cultivate professional relationships that last, there are things you should never be caught doing. Show your strength and stand firm by knowing and adhering to some of your "never's in the workplace". There are things you "never" do in the workplace.

The workplace can be a fun place to be if you enjoy what you do. It is also very refreshing when you work with individuals you get along with. Working to accomplish a project on the "right" team can feel like having a "family" away from home. When people become close personal friends at work, it can sometimes create other issues on the job. Many have tried to carry on relationships in the workplace, but, there always seems to be something that comes up that causes a separation in those initial feelings. For this reason, the most practical rule of thumb could be to steer clear of intimate relationships at work because it only muddies up the workplace waters. Here are a few "never's" to consider in the workplace.

NEVER - Never feed negativity in the workplace. People that are looking to sabotage your positive efforts may want information about you and what you do to create a negative light. Always guard information on a "need to know" basis.

Be cautious! Find out why people need the information they are seeking before you give it out. If the coast is clear, fire away. When it is necessary to give out personal and private information at work, remember that your workplace is that; your workplace! Treat it, and those in it professionally. People who have your best interest at heart will get to know "YOU" first and all other information that is personal will be secondary in the relationship.

Remember that Negative Ninja's are itching to get any information they feel can be used to distort or paint an inaccurate picture of you or someone else. If you need to share in a group setting, share those things that are universal.

NEVER – Never date the boss or anyone else at work. This is crucial! Remember, in the workplace, the company owns your time from the moment you step through their doors until you leave at the end of your work day. It may sound scary, but this is why you receive a pay check each month. Companies expect your best and they should not receive any less.

NEVER – Never be dishonest with others in the workplace. Being dishonest labels you as unworthy of trust. You always want to be trusted in the workplace. This is how you acquire more responsibilities which begets more pay!

NEVER – Never shirk your responsibility at work. If you do this once, you may be labeled as lazy which will not get you front row seats on the promotion board!

NEVER – Never make excuses at work for what you should or could have done. These excuses only benefit you! But, they are only a benefit for a fleeting moment.

NEVER – Never be fake at work. People will always know the real "YOU". Be determined to be "YOURSELF!"

NEVER - Never cloud your career with unhealthy business relationships, because they usually end up disastrous and get you nowhere. The best way to get and stay ahead is to leave all the unnecessary shenanigans outside of work. These are only a few "never's" for the workplace. The most crucial of them all is improper conduct. Many have lost their jobs over improper conduct in the workplace.

Before you engage in workplace relationships, find out what your company policies are on relationships at work before being tagged by Cupid's arrow. Regardless of how discrete a relationship at work begins, it always ends up as indiscrete.

If you are dating the boss, by no means think this relationship is private. It may begin that way but will soon become public knowledge. When you are exposed, you will never have any privacy. Any work you do as a subordinate will be scrutinized to the fiftieth power by other employees inside and outside of the department.

If you are the boss, you may very well lose your ability to earn the trust and respect of those who report to you. Intimate relationships can cloud your professional judgment. Some may even use your relationship with the other employee as a ploy to soften their workload by "chumming" up to the lady or guy, that is involved.

Either way, a personal relationship will affect you and the team you are on in many ways. Even if you perform well, any recognition will be seen as favoritism if you are compensated because of your relationship with the boss. Although there are rare situations where people actually keep their relationship positive, most of the time it does not fare very well.

The bottom line is, you must do the right thing in the workplace. The only "right" thing is to focus on work. This mindset will help you avoid the pitfalls of possible issues with recognition and promotions. Now you can come up for air...You have taken the plunge, and have been well informed about some do's, don'ts, will and won't's of the workplace. We have explored deep waters, floated in shallow coves, gone clam digging and have come up for air. But, through it all, we have not become shark bait.

"Whew!" Now it's time to consider your C.P.R. list. Take a moment and jot down five C.P.R. relationships you have cultivated over the past 1, 2, 5 or 10 years.

READ THIS BEFORE BEGINNING YOUR LIST. Consider the names of the people that you consider to be in your CPR network. When listing them, most people will consider their parents or siblings. This is not necessarily a bad idea but remember, when you list friends, parents or spouses, consider that these individuals must also be CONNECTED in the new circles you must travel, so consider this list carefully. Also remember that the people on this list will often change as you grow professionally. Many times, there are those in our CPR list that are no longer viable to us. When this happens, the relationship does not end, it simply is docked for a time.

LIST YOUR TOP 5 NAMES ON YOUR C.P.R. LIST

1 ______________________________

2 ______________________________

3 ______________________________

4 ______________________________

5 ______________________________

LIST WHAT YOUR TOP 5 PEOPLE CAN DO TO HELP YOU IF YOU LOST YOUR JOB TOMORROW

1 ______________________________

2 ______________________________

3 ______________________________

4 ______________________________

5 ______________________________

Now that you have listed what each of these people can do to assist you... look back at the list and ask yourself if these things listed will really help you find your way back to new employment? If the answer is no, remove the name and see if you can select someone else. It is important to ensure that these names are true to their works and word that if you needed them to help you in any way you could call upon them.

If you have only cultivated one professional relationship in your career, you have much work to do. You are seriously way behind the eight ball! You need to get to work and catch up fast! If you need assistance, now you have a 1% chance of being revived.

If you have two, you now have doubled your chances of being supported in time of a crisis. But you are hard pressed if only one of the two C,P.R.'s is available. Chop-chop! If you have three, you are in better shape because you now have three plans of attack in case of a crisis. If you have four or five, you are in the best shape because you have "OPTIONS." You are swimming full speed ahead!

Congratulations! You now have a C.P.R. Network! Remember that your C.P.R. Network will grow as you grow in cultivating relationships. You must develop these over time.

You now have what it takes to seek out and cultivate professional relationships for your work life balance. You know when and where to plant the seeds so that they will produce the fruits that will be beneficial to you now and later in your career. So, when you acquire this network, you must protect it and never introduce anyone into it that will compromise the integrity of its core.

We have discussed how to identify people for our own C.P.R. network. We know some of the signs that lead up to being fired, and have learned how to prevent a firing from occurring, which is vital for survival in the workplace and knowing when to divulge information at work or when to keep quiet.

Knowing how to identify Negative Ninjas who can harm your career is a must. However, trusting some individuals in the workplace is necessary for survival.

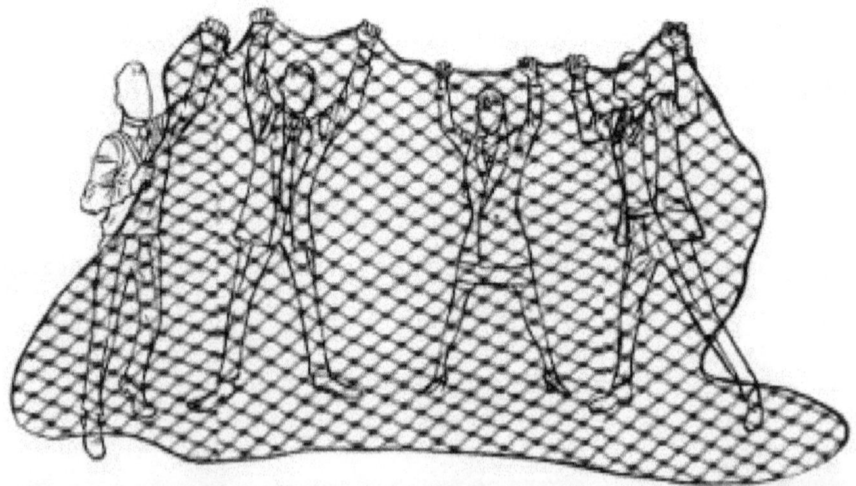

Closing Remarks

With these tips, you are ready to dive into any new workplace or survive in an existing one. Either way, ensure that you use the points in this book as a life vest to stay afloat. If you do not have a C.P.R. network, you must begin cultivating one right now!

Start planting the seeds to build relationships that you can cultivate for your future safety net for workplace survival. Look for people to bring into your network that can reinforce your positive goals in a time of need, but more importantly, be the same kind of person that is sought out by others for the same reason.

Keeping ourselves relevant in the workplace is the key to providing professional assistance to others. Knowing C.P.R. really saves lives...especially in the workplace. Now you are able to relax! You are Top Notch! You can float in safe and secure waters!

Happy Working!

Quote

"A true leader's misconceptions will be quickly aborted before they can give birth to lies."

– Victoria E. Kain

"DO YOU KNOW C.P.R.?"
Cultivating Professional Relationships

The above book title was first published in California, and may be available for purchase at Barnes & Noble, Walmart, Amazon, Itunes, Kindle or through other Distributors. Due to promotion or regional zoning, this title may not be immediately available at your favorite retail store. You may contact Fycore Publishing to order copies or additional copies in other formats. Organizations with orders exceeding more than 100 copies will have a 90 day net Invoice available.

"Do You Know C.P.R.?" is available in these formats:

CD (Audio Book)	$14.95
Soft Back	$13.95
MP3 (Audio Book)	$12.95
Kindle	$11.95
PDF Download	$10.95

Hardback *$129 V.E.K. Series - Collector's Edition*

This VEK series is a keepsake collectible and Includes: 1 Autographed Hardback Color copy | 1 Soft Back, |1 CD of the title **Do You Know C.P.R.** ? by Author Victoria E. Kain with Bonus previews.

For all Inquiries or additional orders:

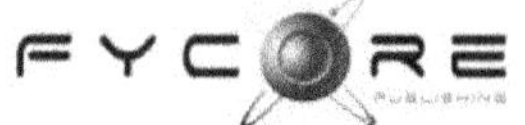

131 Sunset Ave Ste E#353
Suisun City CA, 94585
Office | (800) 470-FYCORE
Facsimile: | (800) 531-0190
Email: | inquiry@fycore.com

Fycore Publishing and Fycore.com are subsidiaries of Gritanium LLC.

Quote

"A lack of clarity and understanding creates a London fog."

– Victoria E. Kain

ABOUT FYCORE PUBLISHING

Fycore Publishing is a next generation Publisher for the 21st Century. What makes us different from other Publishers is that we present great opportunities for Writers & Authors, while cutting the fat and getting down to business on all valid submissions. Our group has Investors affiliated with Movie Industry Executives who sift through the literary forum in hopes to turn good books into movies.

Fycore Publishing is affiliated with organizations and corporations that encourage investments for new projects. Fycore Publishing markets, promotes, publishes and distributes worldwide in multiple languages. Upon review of all manuscripts, should our panel score any submissions we receive above 80%, we will offer a full Investment publishing deal that includes an advance royalty payment, to the Author and a share in percentages of all sales. All other submissions that score under 80%, we offer options below in order to build a publishing relationship. *See contract for details.*

Option 1 Sell your manuscripts outright for a onetime flat fee

Option 2 Fycore Publishing will partner and share all profits

For more information Visit our website

www.fycore.com

SUBMISSIONS

Fycore Publishing created an International IPAN system that protects the legal rights of all parties, virtually eliminating frivolous claims, and simultaneously weeds out persons who are not serious about their manuscripts. We will not accept any unsolicited submissions or materials, and delete, discard and ignore all inquires or questions that do not have an IPAN number affixed on the outside of any U.S. mail packages, or in email subject lines. A person can obtain a unique and distinct IPAN number from our welcome kit, which is only available through our website. Whether you are a beginner or advance Writer / Author, we are the Publishing Company that can help you. Please visit our website today.

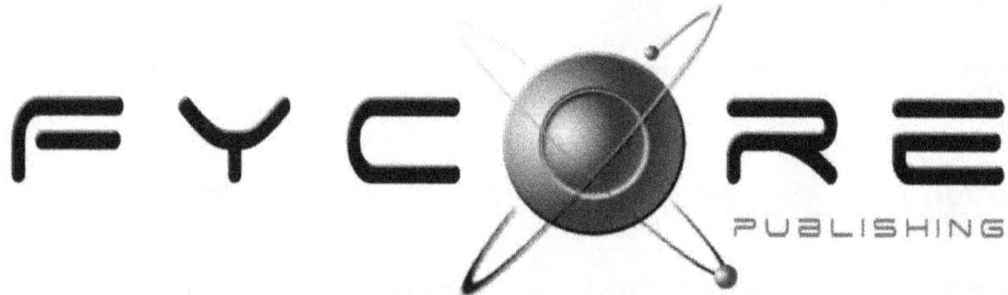

www.fycore.com

Quote

"Bragging rights: The 21 Century form of psychological bullying."

– Victoria E. Kain

Very Special thanks to

- Fycore Inc
- Davis Films
- American Express
- Home Depot
- gritography.com
- Lane Bryant
- Walmart
- Betrlifehcg.com
- Chase
- Gritanium LLC
- GMC
- Amazon.com
- Barnes & Nobel
- Apple Inc.

Quote

"Honesty is the best insurance policy especially if you are the beneficiary."

– Victoria E. Kain

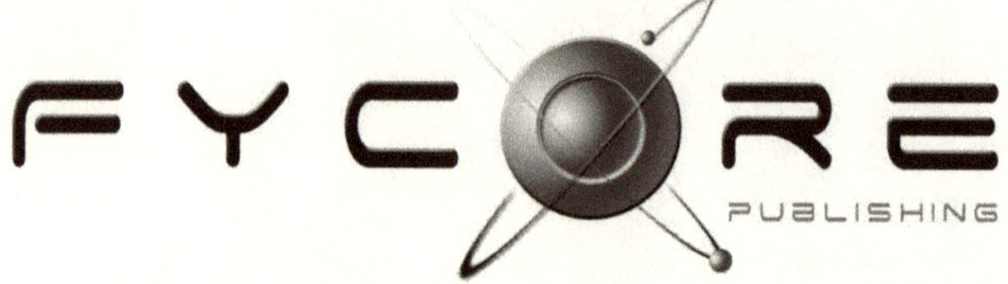

www.fycore.com

ISBN 161910000-2

Quote

"A person will become successful after they believe they can do the things they imagine."

– Davis

1st Book Edition from the

" I'll Be Brief " Series

" Read with ease and understanding "

Arnell Lane Hall

Victoria E. Kain

www.ingramcontent.com/pod-product-compliance
Lightning Source LLC
La Vergne TN
LVHW011405080426
835511LV00005B/416